islands and lagoons of Venice

You live as sea birds with your homes dispersed like the Cyclades across the surface of the water. The solidity of the earth on which they rest is secured only by osier and wattle; yet you do not hesitate to oppose so frail a bulwark to the wildness of the sea. Your people have one great wealth—the fish that suffices for them all. Among you there is no difference between rich and poor; your food is the same, your houses are all alike. Envy, which rules the rest of the world, is unknown to you. All your energies are spent on your salt fields; in them lies your prosperity and your power to purchase those things which you have not. For though there may be men who have little need of gold, yet none live who desire not salt. Be diligent, therefore, to repair your boats, which, like horses, you keep tied up at the doors of your dwellings.

Cassiodorus *writing to the Tribunes or Governors of the Venetian Lagoon settlements—A.D. 525*

The Vendome Press
New York Paris Lausanne

islands and lagoons of Venice

with 160 photographs in full color by **fulvio roiter**

and text by **peter lauritzen**

© 1978 Magnus Edizioni SPA, Udine
English translation © 1980 The Vendome Press, New York City
Distributed in the United States of America by
The Viking Press, 625 Madison Avenue, New York, N.Y. 10022
Distributed in Canada by Penguin Books Canada Limited

All rights reserved. No part of the publication may be
reproduced or transmitted in any form or by any means,
electronic or mechanical, including photocopy, recording
or any information storage and retrieval system,
without permission in writing from the publisher.

Library of Congress Cataloging in Publication Data

Roiter, Fulvio, 1926–
   Islands and lagoons of Venice.

   The photos. were published in 1978 in an Italian ed.
with text by G. Parisi under title: Laguna.
   1. Venice—Description—Views.   2. Venice, Lagoon of
—Description and travel—Views.   I. Lauritzen, Peter.
II. Title.
DG674.7.R62   779′.994531   80–50852
ISBN 0–86565–001–2
Printed and bound in Italy

Contents

1 The Valli of the Venetian Lagoon *6*

2 Lio Piccolo Vignole Sant' Erasmo *41*

3 Mazzorbo Torcello Altino Burano
San Francesco del Deserto *61*

4 Murano San Michele *97*

5 The Lido Malamocco Alberoni
San Lazzaro degli Armeni
San Pietro in Volta Pellestrina *117*

6 Chioggia *169*

Historical Notes *189*

Notes on the Photographs *193*

Technical Notes *200*

1 The Valli of the Venetian Lagoon

The Venetian Lagoon lies on the map like a crescent, the cusp pointing to the east, extending from the mouth of the Sile River in the north to the Brenta in the south. A flat calm of brackish water covers some 212 square miles, an area protected from the Adriatic Sea by a thin, attenuated atoll of sand and mud, a littoral reef whose name—Lido—long ago entered the hybrid vocabulary of cosmopolitan Europe. There are few immutable facts about the Lagoon, and as much as half of its extent is submerged only occasionally. But the chief characteristics of this ecological phenomenon are change and light, water and land. The Lagoon quite simply remains one of the most extraordinarily suggestive and varied natural environments yet to be found in Europe, and although apparently still in its primitive condition, it has spawned upon a cluster of mud-flat islands the greatest city-state in European history.

The Lagoon was born of opposing forces, and its tenuous survival continues to be governed by contradiction. In the aeons of prehistory, the Sile and Brenta rivers slowly pushed tons of silt and sand to the sea, creating an alluvial flow that was gradually arrested by the tides that rise and fall in the upper end of the Adriatic. The sea shored up the rivers' sludge and sand and formed the Lido reef. However, the Lido was never an unbroken barrier, and today the sea can enter and withdraw through three openings, filling and emptying separate tidal basins. The records of Venetian history indicate that as many as eight entrances once gave access to the Adriatic, although nature has now erased all trace of them. Paradoxically, it was the actions and design of men that channeled and directed the forces of nature. Eager to preserve and protect the living Lagoon, the Venetian Republic diverted the mouths of the rivers that emptied into it and thus prevented the watery fields from becoming a malarial marshland. The Venetians also undertook sophisticated and complex engineering to ensure that the tides were free to flow in, spread over, and scour the labyrinthine channels of their habitat.

Seawater enters twice daily through the three *porti* at the Lido and follows a mainstream that, on occasion, runs as fast as 3 miles per hour, digging a natural channel some 30 feet deep. The mainstream, known as the "trunk," divides into "branches," or *rami*, and eventually into the even more treelike ramifications called *ghebi*, characteristic of a tidal force diminished from the effort to reach the Lagoon's farthest limits. These myriad tidal streams and rivulets cut through the *barene,* or "clay flats," near the shoreline (4). By definition the *barene* are not covered by the normal tidal influx. Absorbing the small amount of fresh water that infiltrates along the mainland shore, they become fertile ground for tamarisk, sea lavender, and the cane brakes that are a refuge and nesting area for Lagoon birds (6–9). Farther from the shore and exposed only at low tide, the Lagoon's shoals have a different name—*velme* (2)—and are primarily sandy in composition. Barren of vegetation, they nonetheless provide the natural breeding ground for the Lagoon's crustaceans: the famous Venetian shrimp—*scampi*—or the *granzeola* crab. The navigable channels through these shoals are marked by *bricole* (15), clusters of three tall piles sunk along the edge of the channel and varied only at the intersection of two channels where a taller pile indicates the junction. In the 16th century, it was calculated that over 140,000 *bricole* were used in the Lagoon.

But the Venetians have marked the Lagoon with more than the *bricole* of the navigable waterways. In the flats and marshes near the shore, stake palisades driven into the Lagoon bed and packed with hard *barene* clay outline the *valli da pesca*. These precincts were devised as fish traps. In summer *cefalù* (mullet), *branzino* (sea bass), *orate* (John Dory), and eels migrated towards the brackish areas from the Adriatic, where evaporation made the highly saline (37 percent) seawater intolerable. As the fish entered the Lagoon, sluice gates were opened to channel them into the *valli*. There the captive fish fed throughout the summer, moving back towards the sea in the autumn, when the Lagoon's shallows and the *valli* cooled rapidly. Well grown, sluggish, and massed together, the fish were now easy to net and send off to market.

In Venetian dialect, the word *valle* describes both these primitive yet sophisticated fisheries and also the large tracts of channels and *barene* owned and used for duck shooting (12–14). The best *valli da caccia* are located in the northern Lagoon nearest the paths of the winter migration. The Venetians of the Republic practiced duck shooting with bow and arrow, and the Doge owned all the birds shot in the Valle di Marano. Each year at Christmas he was required to present a brace of ducks, one fat and one lean, to every member of the patriciate. This obligation became increasingly difficult to fulfill, and in 1521 the Great Council permitted the Doge to substitute a silver medal called *Osella,* the dialect word for "bird." The cane brakes still camouflage patient duck shooters waiting in their punts in the chill winter dawn of the northern Lagoon, and even now the reeds of the *barene* are cut to make thatched shelters for shallow-draft fishing boats, just as they once provided roofing for the houses in the *valli.* At one time or another Venetians have turned every detail of their otherwise barren environment to practical purpose or profit. In the 18th century, they found in the brakes (18, 19) the raw material for elegant cane-backed chairs and for the surfaces of their most beautifully frescoed ceilings. Suspended on iron hooks from palace and church ceiling beams, reed matting could often be curved to suggest vaulting. A smooth coat of plaster made it ready for the exquisite painting of such masters as Ricci, Piazzetta, and Giambattista Tiepolo. In addition to cane and reed, Venetians still harvest small trees (23, 32) for the Lagoon's staked nets and mussel lines (22). The stakes also serve to mark off the *valli da pesca,* just as the Lido's fir and pine forests once yielded the raw material for channel markers, for roof and ceiling beams, as well as for the very foundations of the great metropolis that rose on the high-banked mud flats in the center of the Lagoon.

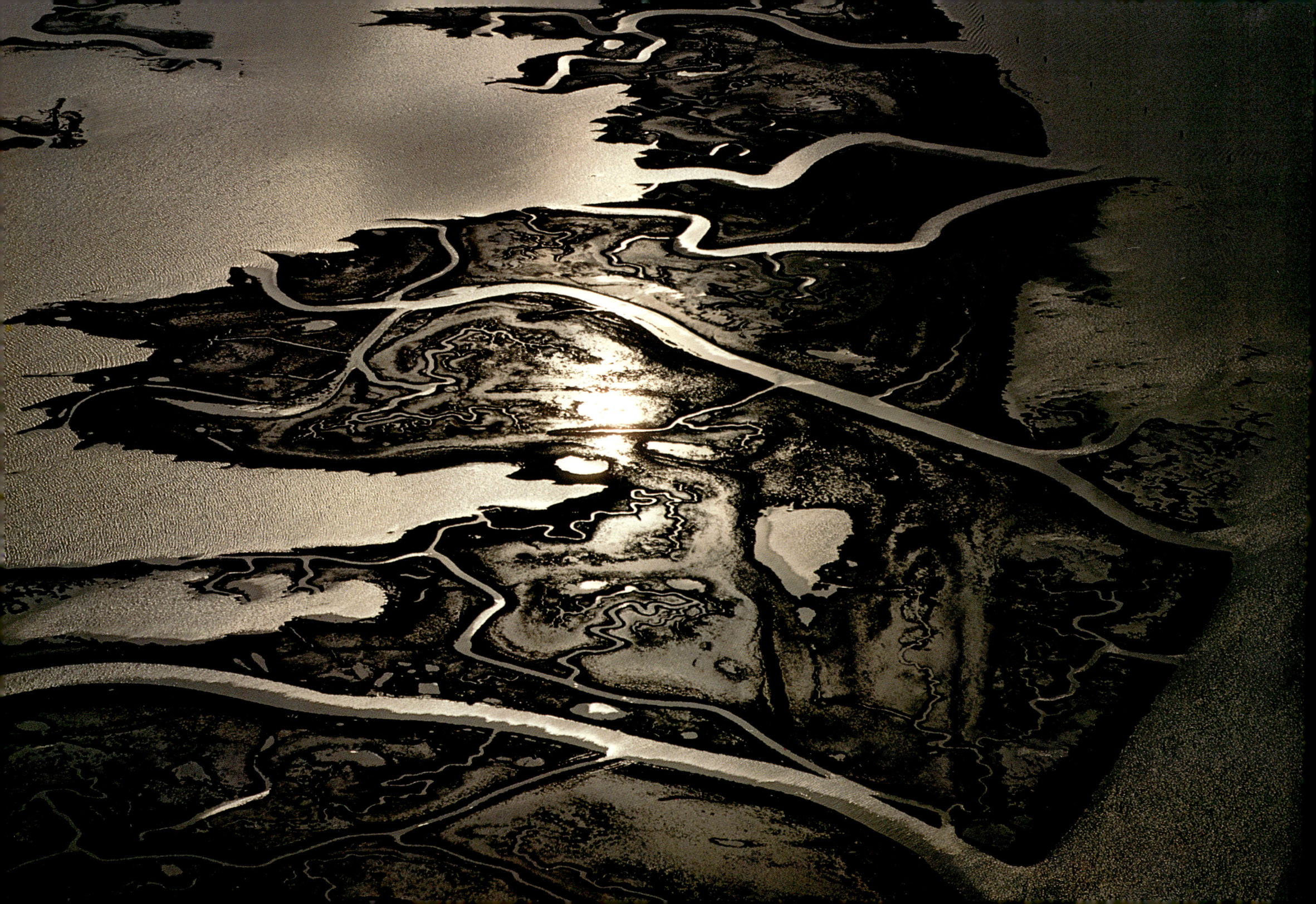

2 Lio Piccolo
Vignole
Sant' Erasmo

The Lagoon presents many varied contrasts with the city it embraces. Where Venice is often closed and secretive behind brick and crumbling plaster, the reaches of its surrounding water are open. Yet in its own way the Lagoon also remains mysterious and unapproachable, while Venice publicly glories in its theatrical qualities. The Lagoon is empty, the city crowded. The essence of both is light, but in the city it is the reflected and refracted light of highly polished, jewellike surfaces, mirrors, and mosaic, silk, gold leaf, satin, and marble. The Lagoon's colors are as diffuse as its horizons; yet for the eye tired of stone and stucco, the islet-studded waters seem filled with the vivid hues of growing things. Even the most built-over islands have open fields of green grass, and the market-garden islands (34, 36), in their proper season, provide the richest contrast with the metropolis. The most fertile and protected lie on the Lagoon side of the Lido's northernmost stretch. The village of Lio Piccolo (34)—the "Small Lido"—is reached by a deep-water channel cutting through *valli*, marshes, and *barene* covered in summer with purple sea lavender (35). It also flows by reaches of salt fields (*saline*), which, although now abandoned, provided a staple of Lagoon commerce for centuries and led the Venetians to dominate the river routes of the Italian mainland as well as the coastal trade of the lagoons. Salt panning in the Lagoon became a state monopoly and an immense source of revenue, for throughout Europe salt was not only highly prized as a seasoning but also widely used to preserve meat.

While the Republic organized the efficient and profitable working of the salt fields, the local fishermen supplemented their livelihood and their diet with what they could grow in the islands. An ancient food, the humble bean is grown in the Veneto in such colorful variety and abundance (38, 39) as to contribute the famous thick bean soup—*pasta fasoi*—to traditional Venetian cuisine. A more refined crop is the artichoke (41), which flourishes in the Lagoon's foggy climate (40). During the late 15th century it was sufficiently prized and admired to provide a handsome design for the silks, brocades, and damasks of Renaissance robes. By that time the Venetians had acquired a considerable mainland empire, and throughout the following century the Republic encouraged the serious pursuit of agriculture, which entailed land reclamation, scientific cultivation, and the introduction of crops from the New World. The market gardeners of the islands followed suit, and the *Pomo*

Lio Piccolo
Vignole
Sant' Erasmo

d'Oro, the "Golden Apple" of the Hesperides, or tomato, became a staple crop in the Lagoon (45). *Grano turco,* maize or Indian corn, was widely planted within the decade after its discovery in 1492 on the island of Cuba (37). Throughout Europe maize served for fodder, but in the Veneto *grano turco* is ground into a meal, cooked, and eaten under a name borrowed from the Roman legionnaires' *pulmentum.* Golden yellow *polenta,* made of maize and cooked in a variety of ways, replaced the less nutritious millet *(setaria italica)* cakes that had been the mainstay of the peasant diet. As a component of classic Venetian cuisine, *polenta* is traditionally served with wild duck, fish, or eels from the Lagoon, with quail shot in the fields on the shore, or with the facetiously named *osei scampai* ("escaped birds") made of veal or sausages.

Venetian cooking is not the richest nor the most imaginative, and in the Lagoon the local diet consists mainly of freshly caught and simply prepared fish. But the markets at the Rialto and those scattered throughout the Lagoon present wonderfully colorful displays of an amazing variety of vegetables, fruit, and other produce. For centuries things common to the Venetian markets seemed extraordinarily exotic. In 1611 the English traveler Thomas Coryate avidly described all he could to his readers: ". . . they have another excellent fruite called Anguria, the coldest fruite in taste that ever I did eate: the pith of it, which is in the middle, is as redde as blood, and full of blacke kernals. They finde a notable commodity of it in sommer, for the cooling of themselves in time of heate. For it hath the most refrigerating vertue of all the fruites in Italy." *Anguria* (46) is still grown in the islands and eaten during the summer, although as watermelon it no longer seems foreign in taste and appearance to the English-speaking world.

The Venetians, however, never thought of their Lagoon as an extended market garden developed, planted, cultivated, or fished merely to feed the population of the capital. To the citizens of the Most Serene Republic—that is, to the region's occupants for more than a thousand years—the Lagoon was their impregnable defense and protection: *sacros muros patriae* ("the sacred bulwark of the fatherland"). The first refugees to seek sanctuary there joined scattered natives who had fished these waters from time immemorial and who had worked the Lagoon's salt pans for the inhabitants of the Roman mainland. The settlers of the 5th century introduced the trappings of urban life:

class divisions based upon trade and prosperity; a religion governed by bishops ready to build cathedrals and monasteries under even the most adverse conditions; and a sense of political community. Over several centuries these elements developed and coalesced in a Lagoon confederation that eventually, under episcopal supervision, elected a common leader, the *dux* or *doge*. In the meantime, the new arrivals adapted every physical feature of the Lagoon to their needs: the clay of the *barene* for firing into brick; the reeds for thatched roofs; the pine forests for beams, foundation piling, and the construction of shallow-bottom boats to carry an early river trade in wood and salt. To all this they added fragments of stone and marble decoration brought from the ravaged and devastated sites of their mainland homes. They also contributed their knowledge of commerce and their experience of religious and political organization.

The seven legendary churches built by the bishop Saint Magnus on seven different islands were followed by cathedrals and baptistries, as well as by the monasteries where communal agriculture served as a model for self-sufficiency in the islands. And it was not long before the inhabitants found the Lagoon suitable to another industry besides salt mining. The fine sands of its shores inspired them to emulate the Roman talent for firing, modeling, and blowing glass. All this was accomplished gradually over a long period of time. Venice's legendary foundation on March 25 in A.D. 421 dated from the consecration of a church dedicated to Saint James and built on one of the high-banked islands *(Rivo Alto/Rialto)* at the center of the Lagoon. Yet the hundred odd islands clustered around San Giacometto di Rialto became the capital of the Lagoon confederation only in 811, when the tenth Doge transferred his government there from the Lido. The earliest centuries of the Venetians' existence in the Lagoon do not belong to the settlement at the Rialto, but rather to the island communities scattered across its northern reaches and to those gathered at its edge on the Lido.

3 Mazzorbo
Torcello
Altino
Burano
San Francesco del Deserto

The northern Lagoon played an important role in this part of Venice long before the barbarian invasions and the foundation of the city itself. Navigable channels brought ships across the Lagoon from the Adriatic to Altinum (Altino), the third richest commercial emporium, after Aquileia and Patavium (Padua), in the Roman province of Venetia-Histria. The great network of Roman roads gave Altinum its importance in northeastern Italy. The Via Popilia ran through its center, coming from Ravenna along the edge of the Lagoon and leading north to Pannonia and east into Istria. Altinum also stood at the beginning of the Via Claudia Augusta, which followed the Piave River north to its source in the Austrian mountain passes. There was also a road that led from the city directly to Padua. Veneto highways still follow the raised, dead-straight Roman roadbeds that were once paved with large rectangular stone slabs carefully fitted together without cement. Fragments of this paving occasionally survive marking an obsolete route across a remote field (54). This road system held the Roman Empire together until the 5th century, when barbarian tribes crossed the northern borders and descended into Italy to reach Rome.

Altinum's inhabitants escaped from Attila and successive waves of Huns, Goths, and Longobard invaders by fleeing to the sea, or rather into the Lagoon lying between Altinum and the Adriatic. They sought refuge in the barely habitable mud-flat islands scattered among the channels leading to Altinum's seaports (49). It was only after many centuries that the rivers emptying into this part of the Lagoon completely altered its geography. Gradually, as the sea entrances were closed and buried beneath river silt and Lido sand, the islands of Ammiana and Costanziaca, important settlements of the early refugees, vanished altogether beneath tidal waters. Meanwhile, vast open reaches and channels became choked and clogged until they were stagnant breeders of "Evil Air," the malaria that eventually depopulated the earliest settlements.

The most important community established itself on the island of New Altinum, or Torcello (53), as they called it after the mainland watchtower visible across the water. This colony grew to number as many as twenty thousand persons, only for the island to be abandoned some six hundred years ago after endemic malaria had decimated its population. Derelict buildings, ruins, and stone fragments give Torcello a poetically remote and deserted atmosphere completely different from the vivid colors and characteristic activity of nearby Burano (60–67), whose inhabitants can be taken to represent the enduring independence and self-sufficiency of island communities in the northern Lagoon. Burano never became the great commercial emporium nor the ecclesiastical capital that Torcello was. Its humbler prosperity was that of fishermen until the 16th century, when Venice adopted and promoted the local cottage industry as one of Europe's most distinctive luxuries—Burano lace (68, 69). Contemporary taste and fashion have drastically reduced the number of lacemakers still at work on Burano, although the island's menfolk persevere in the fishing that is as old as the Lagoon itself.

The refugee settlers did not merely swell the native population of fishermen. They contributed their commercial expertise and prosperity, their sense of municipal as opposed to tribal community. Furthermore, they came to settle in the islands under the guidance of their bishops. Richly embellished church buildings (56–59) still stand as monuments to their piety and their urban prosperity. High dignitaries, including the Byzantine emperor's mili-

Mazzorbo
Torcello
Altino
Burano
San Francesco del Deserto

tary governor, witnessed the consecration of the cathedral at Torcello in 639, and the relics of more than one sainted bishop were enshrined beneath its altars. By the year of the millennium, the Venetians had revived seaborne trade with the outposts of what had once been the Roman Empire: Dalmatia, the Peloponese and the Greek archipelago, Alexandria and the Levant. Pious Venetian merchants returned home with more sacred relics for the Republic's churches; the Doges' nephews and sons held rich benefices in the islands and saw to the suitably sumptuous decoration of their cathedrals. Torcello's splendid pavements and golden mosaics reflect this wealthy patronage, while the cathedral building itself survives as a monument to the Church's role in consecrating the northern Lagoon as a sanctuary from barbarism. Called an "Ark of Refuge" by Ruskin, this beautiful structure is now marooned and abandoned save for its custodian and the Sunday tourists.

The Lagoon preserves much that belongs to an earlier, prehistoric, almost legendary past. Stretches of *barene* survive to suggest the original appearance of Venice itself, while fishing communities like Burano and those farther south recall the Lagoon's original inhabitants who rescued Saint Mark himself from shipwreck. The Evangelist was on a mission to this corner of Italy where he charged Saints Hermargorus and Fortunatus to found the diocese of Aquileia. According to local tradition, he was brought, following rescue, to some remote island where he lay down to sleep and heard the words *Pax tibi Marce, evangelista meus*, revealing that one day Mark would rest forever among the Venetian islands. The chronicles relate how in 828 two fishermen from Torcello and Malamocco fulfilled the prophecy by bringing the relics of Venice's patron saint to the Lagoon from Alexandria in Egypt.

The Lagoon's fishermen, their trade, and their water craft are the living link with those legendary times. The same shallow-bottom boats cross tide-covered shoals (53); heavier craft ply the marked channels under painted sails whose designs proclaim their owners' island and even their clan (73). The local rowed boats are equally distinctive, for among the hundreds of different sizes and traditional shapes, all are rowed by oarsmen who stand facing the bows (76, 77). The long oars rest in the carved crook or socket of the *forcola*, a walnut oarlock, and on the smaller boats this fulcrum assumes a twisted form whose every crook can be used for maneuvering leverage while the oarsman barely shifts his stance. The larger boats are never handled with such finesse, and their *forcole* are mere stubby pivots set close to the deck (77). Every form of Venetian rowing and all the traditional Lagoon craft appear in the *vogalonga,* the annual 20-mile rowing marathon, while the pastel-colored racing gondolas—the *gondolini* (75)—compete in a series of regattas held throughout the year. But the *sandola* (53) remains the classic Lagoon rowboat, a small skiff that the lone fisherman rows with two oars held cross-wristed *alla valesana* ("in the *valli* fashion").

The regattas are occasions for festivity everywhere in the Lagoon, although Burano undeniably provides the most appropriately colorful backdrop. The vivid hues of the houses make Burano's quays and *calli* a rich patchwork on the faintly marked Lagoon horizons, which are otherwise accented only by the dark streaks of barren mud flat. Slender leaning spires and sturdy, blunt bell towers occasionally break the Lagoon's low-lying silhouette, and across from Burano a strip of tall, dark cypress trees marks the site of another legendary shipwreck. It was here in 1220 that Saint Francis, returning to Italy from his mission in Syria, found himself the victim of the Lagoon's violent and unpredictable storms. He reached shelter on an uninhabited island not far from Burano where the birds and animals recognized him and provided a delighted and fraternal welcome. Thrusting his staff into the barren soil, Saint Francis claimed the deserted shoal for himself and his brethren. Today the Friars of San Francesco del Deserto (78, 79) show visitors the immense cypress tree that miraculously sprang full-grown from their patron's staff.

Crossing the Lagoon on the water buses (81), first introduced to bring Venice closer to its remote islands, the visitor is ferried from one world to another. The ponderous iron boats are filled in summer with tourists, but on a winter day their well-heated cabins may hold only a few passengers, perhaps a monk from San Francesco del Deserto (52) and a few island housewives returning from a shopping expedition. But as in any community, the *vaporetti* are crowded to overflowing early every weekday morning and again in the evening as the "rush hour" takes the modern Lagoon dweller across the silent stretches of calm water to and from their jobs in Venice or in the factories of Murano.

4 Murano
San Michele

Murano, like Torcello, Mazzorbo, and Burano, began life as a haven from the 5th-century barbarian incursions into the Roman Empire's northern provinces. The first refugee settlers came primarily from Altinum, but the town they established is not an abandoned relic of a glorious past, nor does it survive by reverting to dependence upon the Lagoon's natural resources. Quite simply, Murano perpetuates its ancient native industry right into the 20th century, despite the changes and chances of taste and fashion. In fact, the local glass factories (82, 90–93) have remained the Lagoon's only industry since the closure of Venice's great Arsenal shipyards following the collapse of the Republic in 1797. When Henri III of France visited *la Serenissima* in 1574, the Arsenal's thousands of workmen could build, fit out, and launch a fighting ship in a single day, but it was to Murano that the King was taken to see the fantastic creations of Venice's most highly evolved traditional craft. Surviving examples of early Murano glass embody extraordinary skill and artistic talent (92), and it was no mere coincidence that in the mid-15th century Murano fostered Venice's first "school" of important individual painters. Among them the Vivarini family maintained their association with the island's manufacture of glass, and in 1521 Alvise Vivarini's daughter, Armenia, obtained the exclusive privilege or patent for the design and fabrication of the rare and exquisite glass galleons that ornamented the most festive Venetian banquet tables. Few examples of these fragile creations survive, and even the oldest single dated piece of Murano glass goes back no further than the mid-15th century. However, this piece, a delicately embellished dark saphire-blue wedding cup, not only demonstrates a skilled revival of ancient Roman enameling on glass, but also preserves the name of the master craftsman who created it: Angelo Barovier.

Baroviers still work at Murano, but even more remarkable are the genealogical charts that trace Angelo's forbears all the way to the 13th century, when, by government decree, all Venice's glass furnaces were transferred to Murano as a precaution against the perennial threat of fire in the city. From that time onward the master glassblowers' names were recorded in a registry every bit as exclusive as the Golden Book of the Venetian patriciate. But Murano's history recedes into an even more remote and splendid past embodied in her cathedral, a building reconsecrated, according to legend, at the behest

Murano
San Michele

of Otto III, the Emperor of the West (84–86). In the following century it was enlarged as the shrine for Saint Donatus' relics (including bones of the dragon he slew) and decorated with arcaded apse galleries that are unique in Venice. Very few of the seventeen parish churches built on Murano's five islands remain, and virtually nothing survives of the great convents and monasteries where the Doges' womenfolk withdrew from the world and where monumental ducal tombs were erected. Vanished too, except for fragments, are the hundreds of villas and palaces that once made Murano the most popular of patrician retreats.

In the early 16th century, when the island's population reached thirty thousand, some of Venice's richest families laid out extensive and elaborately ornamented garden parterres with small *casini* (pleasure pavilions) to which the owners and their guests could retire for informal entertainments. Here they listened to lute and madrigal concerts, engaged in Platonic dialogue and philosophical discussion, recited poetry, and staged amateur theatricals based upon the texts of classical antiquity. Daniele Barbaro, the editor and commentator of Vitruvius, collaborated with Andrea Palladio to build a palace for the Trevisan family and then brought Paolo Veronese and Alessandro Vittoria to Murano to decorate the interior. The *arbiter elegantarum* of written Italian, Cardinal Pietro Bembo, frequented learned circles at Murano. So did Pietro Aretino, the scourge of princes, who was often to be found with his friend Titian in the company of the patrician Andrea Navagero. An accomplished poet in Latin, Navagero carried on serious botanical studies in the garden he laid out on Murano.

All trace of these gardens has disappeared, and only vestiges of faded fresco and bits of ruined statuary suggest what Palazzo Trevisan was once like. The 16th-century *casino* of the Mocenigo family is buried in a labyrinth of delapidated and derelict factory buildings that once housed the Venetian *Contarie*. In the 16th and 17th centuries the *Contarie* factories of Murano were organized to produce the glass beads used for trade and barter in the course of early voyages of exploration throughout the world. Murano's beads have been found on every continent touched by European explorers. The island's glass industry enjoyed a great renaissance in the 18th century when silvered and incised mirror glass, elaborate table decorations, and brightly colored, convoluted chandeliers were added to the earlier repertory of beads, counterfeit gemstones, goblets, chalices, and platters—in addition to those airy crystal confections with finely wrought stems and handles whose practical purpose defies all rational analysis. During this period Murano's popularity as a pleasure resort was undiminished, as Casanova attests in his amusing account of a rendezvous there with the French ambassador's mistress, who was also, incidentally, the abbess of one of the island's great convents.

On the way to and from Murano, Casanova's gondola passed two small monastery islands. San Cristoforo vanished in the 19th century as completely as did the gardens and pleasure pavilions Casanova frequented on Murano. But nearby the monastery church dedicated to Saint Michael still stands and serves the remaining island, which, according to a plan devised by Napoleon and later executed by the Austrians, was made up of the two original pieces of land and transformed into Venice's municipal cemetery, San Michele. Countless legends have attached themselves to this "Island of the Dead," most of them ignoring the fact that its origins, by Venetian standards, are very recent. An undeniably romantic atmosphere surrounds the graves of such eminent artists as Diaghilev, Stravinsky, and Ezra Pound. The poor of Venice, meanwhile, are buried here only to have their bones exhumed after a decade, which relieves their families of the expense of monuments. Exhumation also permits San Michele's limited ground to be reused. In their final resting place the bones of the poor have even more eminent company on an island ossuary, Sant'Arrian, in the northern Lagoon. There they join the bones and ashes taken from the despoiled and desecrated ducal tombs opened by Napoleon's agents in unwitting fulfillment of his infamous vow to be "an Attila for the Venetian state."

5 The Lido
Malamocco
Alberoni
San Lazzaro degli Armeni
San Pietro in Volta
Pellestrina

Attila's invasion and successive barbarian attacks upon the northern Roman Empire drove refugees to the Lido as well as to Murano, Torcello, Burano, and the other islands of the Lagoon. When citizens of Roman Patavium (Padua) sought sanctuary at Malamocco, the Lido was an atoll (97) of at least half a dozen islands, and Metamauco existed as the mainland city's seaport. Maritime cargo was unloaded there and sent in shallow-draft lighters across the Lagoon to the mouth of the Bacchiglione River, whence it was towed upstream to Padua. Originally, Padua served mainly as a junction of overland trade. Its prosperity did not come from the sea, and the Lido bore little resemblance to its present state. In the 5th century, and indeed until only a hundred years ago, the Lido's entire length was forested with *pinus pinea,* the "umbrella pine" that flourishes in the sandy soil of the Mediterranean coasts. What Dante called *la divina foresta* was jealously protected by the Venetians ever since the Lido plantations were first used as material for building houses and ships. Piling cut from these trees and from conifers felled and rafted down rivers to the Lagoon virtually petrified in brackish water. Short, widely spaced piles driven into the mud flats supported immense structures like the Piazza San Marco's tall watchtower, which rose above the new Rialtine city and acted as a beacon to Venetian shipping for over a thousand years.

The Campanile was begun late in the 9th century after the Venetians had survived the first attack on their Lagoon sanctuary. The Frankish king Pepin's capture of Malamocco forced them to abandon the Lido and to take refuge on the Rialtine islands. From there, over five hundred years later, the Venetians withstood the only other invasion ever attempted from the Lido. Tradition recounts that Pepin was ultimately defeated by a combination of Venetian cunning and the treacherous nature of the Lagoon. In 1379 these were again the basic ingredients of Venetian survival, although the War of Chioggia brought the Republic closer than ever before, or after, to complete disaster. The Lagoon was Venice's impregnable defense for a millennium until April 1797, when the French frigate, *Libérateur d'Italie,* sailed past the Lido's defenses, was fired upon from the fortress of Sant'Andrea (99), and became the *causis belli* that led directly to Napoleon's occupation of Venice and the destruction of the Most Serene Republic.

The Lido
Malamocco
Alberoni
San Lazzaro degli Armeni
San Pietro in Volta
Pellestrina

In the early 19th century the Lido's fortress of San Nicolò, past which the ducal *bucintoro* was rowed for the annual "Marriage with the Sea," became a deserted, poetic ruin overlooking vast stretches of pine forest and uninhabited seaside where Lord Byron rode daily in the guise of Shelley's Count Madolo. Only late in the century did a local entrepreneur conceive of turning a profit by introducing the conventions and apparatus of Victorian sea bathing on the Lido. The broad beach of fine sand, the shallow foreshore, and the exceptional clarity of water all contributed to the success of the enterprise and to the Lido's subsequent fame. Soon an international clientele populated the *belle époque* ballrooms of the luxury hotels (110, 111), lending them an exotic note that had its echo in Moorish domes or in Tahitian thatched-roof cabañas (104). Thomas Mann, in *Death in Venice*, describes a jaded, cosmopolitan society at the Grand Hôtel des Bains just before World War I destroyed their Europe. However, the novel's famous vision of death and decadence, conjured up by the sickly imagination of an overwrought hero, is quite at variance with the playground atmosphere of today's Lido. Even the Republic's abandoned fortifications now enclose nothing more sinister than a golf course (112), while the 18th-century seawalls make a path for the local riding club (114). There are still romantic views across the Lagoon to inaccessible or desolate monastery islands (120): Poveglia, where giant tankers lie beached and rusting in the sun (116, 117); or San Lazzaro (126), originally the Republic's "Lazar house," or quarantine hospital, and later the site of an Armenian monastery where Byron once studied. The Lido's ancient Jewish cemetery (119) is still as suggestive as when J.A. Symonds described it in verse as "lost in the dunes, with rank weeds overgrown."

But the Lido's true nature is to be found neither on the sea-swept and eroding beaches nor in the monuments to a dead past, but rather in the relation of the atoll to the Lagoon it created and protects. On the Pellestrina littoral, across the Malamocco sea entrance from the Lido's Alberoni dunes, there are names redolent of ancient Venetian history: Malamocco, the original settlement captured by Pepin in 810 and rebuilt after its destruction by a great tidal wave in 1106; and San Pietro in Volta (131), a tiny fishing village, whose name commemorates Doge Pietro Tribuno's turning back (*volta*) an invasion of Hungarian raiders on Saint Peter's day in 900. The Pellestrina littoral (130), now the thinnest and longest strip of barrier between the Adriatic and the Lagoon, was once interrupted by at least two other entrances to the sea. The Venetians built pallisades out from the shore and altered the tidal currents. In this way they caused the entrances to silt up, which in turn strengthened the current that kept the Chioggia sea entrance deeply scoured. Dykelike land banks protect Pellestrina from the lashing sea storms; behind them the people of this island have laid out market gardens and orchards. There, in vegetable patches and hardy fruit trees, they find supplements to their hard-won income from fishing; also shade from the sultry sirocco sun (141), when summer Sundays bring everyone out to eat, drink, and seek refreshment after the week's work. Brightly painted houses (135) provide a colorful backdrop to their stubby, sturdy fishing trawlers, while behind the quayside village stretches another backdrop: the long, white-bleached Istrian stone wall, which was built by the Venetian Republic to protect Pellestrina when the sea's prevailing winds change into their winter quarter.

130 131

6 Chioggia

The *murazzi,* or "great walls," were built in the mid-18th century to protect the most vulnerable sections of the Lido reef. At the southern end of the Pellestrina littoral, the Lido itself is hardly wider than the seawalls and the roadway behind them (145). After the fall of the Republic, the *murazzi* suffered neglect, and the violent storm of November 4, 1966, battered them with the combined might of gale-force sirocco winds, a sea seiche or tidal wave that struck with momentum built up from across the Adriatic, and a seismic tremor on the seabed. The storm itself would have done sufficient damage, but it also happened to coincide with an exceptional *acqua alta*. When this seasonal "high tide" had risen in the Lagoon, the storm winds prevented its ebb, with the result that the day's second tidal influx was driven in on top of the first, flooding the entire city of Venice to depths of over 6 feet above the mean. This extraordinary concatenation fell upon Venice on precisely the same day that the Arno overflowed its banks, for quite unrelated reasons, and flooded Florence. The damage to countless artistic treasures was horrific, but the world at large remained ignorant of the destruction wrought in the Venetian Lagoon. The *murazzi* were broken and smashed; Sant'Erasmo's fields and market gardens lay under lakes of saltwater, while those on the Lido were ploughed up and swept away by the impact of giant waves; cabañas and piers were torn loose and ripped to shreds and splinters; fishing smacks and heavy trawlers capsized and sank at their moorings. The Lido took the brunt of a cataclysmic storm whose destructive force was barely diminished by the Lagoon's tortuous channels or absorbed by the *barene* and low-lying mud-flat islands. Nonetheless, the Lido and the Lagoon once again saved Venice from devastation, just as in the 14th-century legend where a barque of malignant spirits intent upon ravaging Venice was repulsed by the Lagoon's heavenly protectors: Saint Mark from the Rialtine islands, Saint George from the island of San Giorgio Maggiore, and Saint Nicholas, the patron of mariners and fishermen, from the Lido.

Chioggia is the capital of the Lagoon's fishermen and sailors. For all its superficial similarities with Venice or Burano, Chioggia in the southern Lagoon boasts a strikingly evident independence and individuality. Long before the barbarian invasions of the Roman Empire, a community of fishermen, small traders, and workers of the Lagoon salt pans existed on this island. Chioggia's name, actually of uncertain etymology, has been derived from the *Fossa Clodia,* one of the canals in a network constructed by Roman engineers to link maritime commerce with the rivers of the mainland. Like other scattered settlements in the Lagoon, Chioggia provided a haven from the barbarians, for refugees fleeing Patavium (Padua), Ateste (Este), and the Euganean hills (158) near Mons Silicis (Monselice). The new inhabitants eventually brought Chioggia into the Lagoon confederation, whose capital was first on the Lido at Malamocco and only later transferred to the Rialtine islands under the leadership of their tenth Doge. Drawn up in the mid-9th century, the *Pactum Clodiae* defined the extent of Chioggia's territory, which in 1107 received the bishopric of Malamocco when the original settlement was destroyed by earthquake and tidal wave. At first Chioggia was governed in the Doge's name by a *gastaldo* or "bailiff" and then by a *podestà*, or patrician governor, but although loyal to the Republic, the city's native population remained characteristically independent. They developed a dialect so distinctive that Goldoni described it at length in the preface to his comic masterpiece, *Le Baruffe Chiozzotte* ("Chioggian Quarrels"). Goldoni, who had lived in Chioggia and observed its residents for long periods, noted that virtually all the males were engaged in fishing. Hardly any other trade or social class existed on the island. However, Chioggia was linked with the Lido by a long wooden causeway, and across the narrow inlet a smaller community, Chioggia Minore, grew up characterized by attitudes common to landowners and farmers. Ironically, these two quite different worlds were separated by a stretch of water too narrow to save greater Chioggia from the siege launched across it by the Genoese in 1379.

The War of Chioggia came as the climax to commercial rivalry between Venetian and Genoese merchants trading in the Levant. These quarrels spread to their galley convoys and then erupted into full-fledged naval engagements throughout the eastern Mediterranean. The Venetians pursued the enemy into Genoese waters where, almost a century after the rivalry had flared up in the East, the two fleets exchanged losses and victories. Eventually the Genoese navy entered the Adriatic and, after a signal victory off Istria, moved to attack Venice. Genoese forces captured Chioggia Minore and gained a foothold on the Lido, whence they besieged, captured, and vindictively sacked Chioggia itself. This moment in the War of Chioggia seemed to threaten the imminent defeat and destruction of the Venetian Republic. Widespread panic broke out in Venice, but in the end the Republic was saved by desperate determination, by the resolution and superior strategy of Carlo Zeno, and by the bravery of Admiral Vettor Pisani, who had been released from prison to take command and ultimately to die in battle. Finally, Venice

Chioggia

was saved from siege and defeat by the nature of the Lagoon, but Chioggia had to be sacrificed to the Venetian victory. It never recovered from the hardships of war and the sack by the Genoese.

Chioggians were left to cultivate the natural resources of their surroundings. Today the city is one of Italy's two most important markets and shipping and distribution centers for fish. It handles a volume of produce from the sea twice as large as that of Venice, for example; yet only a fifth of the population are now fishermen (149–156). Many of Chioggia's 25,000 people work in mainland factories or find seasonal jobs across the causeway in the resort hotels that have been built along the Lido beach at Sottomarino, the Chioggia Minore of the Republic. The factories and refineries now grown up around the Republic's fortress at Marghera, swallowing the tiny Lagoon village and staging post of Mestre (158, 159), belong to the history of Italian postwar industrial development. But the expansion of this industrial zone into the Venetian Lagoon poses a threat identical to that recognized in the 16th century by a native of Chioggia, Cristoforo Sabbadino (1487–1560).

The encroachment of reed beds into the Lagoon alerted Sabbadino to the danger of silting brought by mainland rivers. He argued for the diversion of the rivers' mouths so that silt could not strangle the Lagoon's channels, smother the reaches of tidal flats, and thus transform the whole delicate organism into a stagnant, malarial swamp. Healthy circulation could only be maintained by increasing the sweeping and scouring capacity of the sea tides. This was to be done by allowing the Lagoon to extend as far inland as possible. The shore marshes were not to be drained and parcelled out for agriculture. In this, Sabbadino was arguing against a specific scheme for developing the Lagoon's resources proposed in the preceding century by the rich landowner Marco Corner (1412–65). Today the plan is echoed by the proponents of land reclamation in the Lagoon, their purpose being to favor the expansion of Mestre-Marghera's petrochemical refinery and industrial complex.

Fortunately for the Lagoon's survival over the following four centuries, Sabbadino's recommendations were adopted by a government conscious of Venice's debt to the Lagoon. To ensure that the incoming tide had the strength to reach the most distant corners and cover remote tracts, the Republic dredged and widened the three entrances to the sea. Enlarging the Lido *porto,* the Malamocco *porto,* and that at Chioggia permitted an influx sufficient to reach the farthest shore. On the ebb it created a current strong enough to scour the Lagoon's channels and free them from their natural tendency to shoal or silt up. Thereafter the three tidal basins of the Lagoon adjusted their own preservation to the rhythms of the sea, thereby maintaining Venice in a fresh and wholesome environment.

In the first years of the 16th century, the Venetians of the Republic accepted the responsibility for maintaining the hydraulic efficiency of the Lagoon by creating the *Magistrato alle Acque* ("Magistracy of the Waters"). The officials of this agency held extensive powers and meted out drastic punishment to any who interfered with the natural flow of the Lagoon's waters. Presided over by three ranking patricians, the Magistrato included a small deliberative committee and an *inquisitore* or "investigating officer." In addition, the Magistrato was required to seek the opinion of eight specially appointed fishermen whenever their deliberations concerned the Lagoon.

After Napoleon had destroyed the Venetians' government and civilization forever, there remained an admonition to future generations inscribed in 1553 by the Magistrato alle Acque:

VENETORUM URBS
DIVINA DISPONENTE PROVIDENTIA
AQUIS FUNDATA
AQUARUM AMBITU CIRCUMSEPTA
AQUIS PRO MURO MUMITUR.
QUISQUIS IGITUR
QUOQUO MODO DETRIMENTUM PUBLICIS AQUIS
ANFERRE AUSUS FUERIT
HOSTIS PATRIAE JUDICETUR
NEC MINORI PLECTATUR POEMA
QUAM QUI SACROS MUROS PATRIAE
VIOLASSET
HUJUS EDICTI JUS RATUM PERPETUVMQUE
ESTO

(The city of the Venetians / with the aid of Divine Providence / was founded on water / enclosed by water / defended by water instead of walls. / Whoever in any way dares damage the public waters / shall be declared an enemy of the State / and shall not deserve less punishment / than he who breaches the sacred walls of the State / This edict is valid forevermore.)

The Republic recognized and codified the essential paradox of the Venetian Lagoon. It was the defence and protection of their capital from siege and storm; yet it was vulnerable in its every component. It was the birthplace and sanctuary of their great empire and civilization, and it gave life and work to the humblest inhabitants. Yet it had proved to be the breeding ground of disease and death. The Lagoon itself could live or die, but men would survive within it only by studying to preserve and prolong its existence.

Historical Notes

The woodcut map of the Venetian Lagoon was published in 1528 as an illustration in the second volume of Benedetto Bordone's *Isolario*, a treatise on all the islands of the world. It is the oldest printed map of the Lagoon and represents, with fair accuracy, the approximate position of the principal islands in their relation to Venice, to the mainland, and to the Lido. Bordone placed the center of his *rosa ventorum,* or "wind rose," at the heart of Venice's harbor: The Basin of Saint Mark. The central fold of the woodcut gives the map its north-south axis. North is indicated at the top of the double page by a black-tipped arrow, which passes through several islands before touching the mainland shore not far from where Altino (Altinum) would appear on a modern map.

Near the northern edge of Venice's own 117 islands are the twin monastery islets of San Michele and San Cristoforo, joined together in 1837 by the Austrians to make the municipal cemetery of San Michele. Due north is Murano, and still farther north the main channel of the Lagoon passes San Giacomo di Palude ("Saint James in the Marsh") and San Nicolò, later known as the Madonna del Monte. The former was originally a pilgrim hospice; later it became a Cistercian convent and then a Franciscan friary. The church there was deconsecrated in 1810, and during World War I the island became a military installation. San Nicolò was poorer, and after housing various religious communities, it ceased to be inhabited for several centuries. But rechristening came in 1712, after a new church had been built on it and dedicated to the Madonna of the Rosary. Now, once again, ruined walls are all that survive on the island, itself considerably reduced by erosion. The channel north of San Nicolò becomes a canal dividing Mazzorbo in half and leading into the Burano channel, which runs between Torcello and Burano. Not far from Burano on the Lido, Bordone indicates Treporti, the site of one of the Lido's openings to the Adriatic now erased by sand and river silt.

Bordone's northeastern line passes through the crenelated fortifications of the Venetian Arsenal and continues to the Lazzaretto Nuovo ("New Lazar House"). After first serving as a prison for insubordinate militiamen, this island's buildings were converted, during the great plague of 1576, into an auxiliary hospital for contagious diseases. Farther towards the Lido of Cavallino appears the island monastery of San Francesco del Deserto. The point is marked "G" for *Greco* ("Greek"), the northeastern wind that prevails during the Venetian winter.

LIBRO SECONDO XXX

Historical Notes

Following the conventions of Venetian mapmaking, the east is marked with a cross to recall the sun's rising as symbolic of the Resurrection. Just north of Bordone's cross lies the island of the Certosa, the Carthusian order brought from Florence at the suggestion of San Bernardino of Siena. Only a few years after the map was published, Michele Sanmichele designed the fortress of Sant'Andrea to protect Venice's principal entrance to the Adriatic. Bordone depicted a crenelated tower on the Lido to represent the existing fortification of San Nicolò.

In the southeastern quarter of the Lagoon, Bordone drew the island of San Servolo, a monastic establishment dedicated in the 18th century to the care of patrician lunatics. Nearby appear two islands then designated for quarantine, San Lazzaro and the Lazzaretto Vecchio. *Lazzaretto* was a dialect corruption of the island church's dedication to Saint Mary of Nazareth. Originally intended as a pilgrim hospice, the "old" Lazzaretto was transformed into the Republic's first isolation hospital for contagious diseases, a change undertaken on the advice of San Bernardino of Siena. The name San Lazzaro reflects an early association with leprosy, but later the site fell into disuse for several centuries, until 1717 when an order of Armenian Catholic monks took up residence there. They still inhabit the island. The southeastern wind—the Sirocco—blows up the Adriatic from the Sahara and can be considered the prevailing wind of Venice and the Lagoon. The Sirocco line ("S") points to that part of the Pellestrina littoral where the Venetians built palisades into the sea so as to close two shallow and dispensable openings.

Directly south of the northern tip of Venice's long Giudecca Island lies La Grazia, originally no more than a *barena*. This bit of land came into being when garbage was dumped there in 1264; it then served as a way station for pilgrims traveling by Venetian ships to the Holy Land. The church of Santa Maria della Grazia was suppressed and destroyed in 1810. Close by lies San Clemente, which, like so many other Lagoon islands, once harbored a pilgrim hospice, a religious community, and a hospital for the plague-infected. It was from San Clemente that the terrible plague of 1630 spread to Venice. South of San Clemente the island of Santo Spirito was once noted for its church built by Jacopo Sansovino and decorated with paintings by Titian and Palma il Vecchio. For centuries Santo Spirito was where foreign ambassadors were welcomed by a delegation of senators, who then escorted the envoys into Venice for the presentation of their credentials to the Doge. Nearest the Lido is the island of Poveglia, named either for its poplar trees or for the Roman consul Popilio Leno. As the antiquity of its name implies, Poveglia was settled not by monks, but much earlier by refugees fleeing the barbarian invasions of the mainland. Over the centuries Poveglia was reduced by erosion, storms, and earthquakes until finally, in the mid-17th century, the descendants of the original inhabitants refused to remain there. The southern point of the map's *rosa ventorum* is initialed "O" for the Ostro wind and points to the island of Chioggia.

In the southwest quadrant, between the Africo and Ponente winds, lies Sant'Angelo della Concordia, the site of an 11th-century monastery placed under the jurisdiction of San Nicolò del Lido. A succession of different religious orders established themselves there until 1689, when the island was struck by lightning, set afire, and ultimately abandoned. Today the island is known as Sant'Angelo della Polvere for its wartime use as a powder magazine. San Zorzi d'Alega is the Venetian dialect rendering of "Saint George in the Seaweed." It too housed an eminent Benedictine community and was devastated by fire. But after reconstruction in 1717, San Zorzi resumed its importance as a stage on the shortest water route linking Venice with the mainland.

Under the French it became a political prison, and under the Austrians a customs depot and passport-control post.

Between the Ponente, or west wind, and the Maestro, which blows from the northwest, can be found San Secondo, now only a few yards from the railroad causeway built in 1854 to link Venice with *terra firma*. The relics of Saint Secundus were brought to the Benedictine nunnery there in 1237 from Asti in Piedmont. Other religious orders found a haven on the island until 1569, the year the Republic requisitioned it for the safe storage of gunpowder, thus saving the Arsenal from the danger of explosions. Dominican monks returned in the following century and remained until 1824, when the church was deconsecrated and razed to the ground.

Apart from the disappearance of Lido sea entrances and the evacuation of almost all the islands shown on Bordone's map, the area of the Lagoon that has changed beyond recognition since 1528 is that section of the mainland nearest San Secondo. The lone tower of Marghera, which still exists, and the village of Mestre are now completely surrounded by a vast industrial development and crowded by a population almost four times as great as that of today's Venice.

Notes on the Photographs

1. The Lagoon's horizons vanish in the thick mist of a December dawn.

2. At low tide the Lagoon reveals stretches of *velme,* sandy shoals cut through by serpentine natural channels called *ghebi.*

3. The Lagoon's deeper channels often make a remarkably straight path between the vegetated clay flats known as *barene.*

4. The Lagoon's *barene* are often staked out as enclosed areas for the capture of fish migrating from the sea. The fish enter these *valli da pesca* through sluice gates opened and closed at the mouth of long channels leading to the Lagoon's sea entrances.

5. The Lagoon often deceives the unwary and here reveals its shallows only through the reflections of gulls standing on the muddy shoals just below the water's surface.

6. Among the many waterfowl breeding and nesting in remote stretches of the northern Lagoon are splendid examples of the gray heron (*ardea cinerea*), here photographed on an April afternoon.

7. A pair of little egrets wading in the shallow waters of the Val Dogà, recorded with a telescopic lens on an evening in May just before sunset.

8. The snipe, a secretive marsh bird, is extremely difficult to observe closely. The Venetian Lagoon is the snipe's southernmost breeding ground in Europe.

9. Spring is the nesting season for ducks that migrate from the north. Among the Lagoon's many varieties of duck—coot, teal, gadwall, pintail, widgeon, and tufted—the large spoonbill is the most prized and is known as the *germano reale,* the "royal wild duck."

10. An April sunset in the Valle dell'Averto on the western edge of the Lagoon. The Averto *valle* is completely cut off from the rest of the Lagoon by dykes and embankments and covers an area of just over 950 acres.

11. A moorhen in the Valle dell'Averto at sunset. Once open to the tides and used as a *valle da pesca,* this and other enclosed *valli* are now private preserves for duck shooting.

12. Duck shooting in the *valli da caccia* is done from *botte*, duck blinds made from wooden wine casks sunk in the shallows and camouflaged with reeds and marsh grass.

13. A duck hunter and his dog in the Val Dogà wait in one of the shallow draft shooting punts equipped with *forcole*, the carved "oarlocks" used on all Lagoon rowing boats.

14. Duck hunters and their dogs out in the Val Dogà on a January morning. This *valle*, the largest enclosed area in the Lagoon, covers over 4000 acres.

15. A retriever wades among the *barene* with a deep-water channel marked with *bricole* in the background. Further in the distance rises the leaning bell-tower on the island of Burano. The warmer colors are those of an April morning.

16. A January dawn with two duck shooters and their dog in a punt in the Val Dogà. The northern *valli da caccia* are considered the best for hunting since they are nearest the point where migrating ducks first appear in the Lagoon.

17. January hoarfrost on the edges of the southern Lagoon near Chioggia. Fishermen in the background gather clams from the sandy *velme* with long pole-rakes.

18. The cane or reed brakes of the Adige River shore on a sunny February morning. The tall reed grasses, once cut for the thatched roofs of *valle* houses and the frescoed ceilings of Venetian palaces, are still utilized in local craftwork and in some construction.

19. The various reed grasses that flourish in Europe are often planted on the water's edge to convert swamp into dry land, binding the soil with their close, grasslike growth or else with their exceptionally long roots.

20, 21. Houses in the Val Dogà. These were built either on islands or on the perimeter embankments of the *valle*. Most are now abandoned. Like all buildings in the Lagoon, the *valle* houses are constructed of brick on foundations of clay and larch-wood piling.

22. Throughout the southern Lagoon, forests of slender stakes and lines indicate mussel beds. From lines strung across the water's surface hang the *reste* or specially prepared lines to which the mussels attach themselves and grow. In the background is a cabin built on piling for the storage of stakes and lines and for cleaning the harvested mussels.

Notes on the Photographs

23. In recent years, with the *valli da pesca* utilized less efficiently, stake nets have become predominant in the Lagoon's commercial fishing industry. Eel traps, whose different netting systems provide the Lagoon's principal catch, dry in the sun in the background.

24, 25. A fisherman prepares the trammels for use in the Val Dogà. These nets catch fish by trapping them in complicated folds. Here they are laid out on the bow of a *sandolo*, the small fishing boat typical of the Venetian Lagoon.

26. The Lagoon's shallows, like those near Malamocco on the Lido, are ideal ground for setting out fixed fish-traps made of stake nets.

27. A fisherman of the Val Dogà examines and repairs his old nets behind a curtain of new net that may last two years. Sea bass (*branzino*), John Dory (*orate*), and different fish of the mullet family (*cefali*) are caught in the Lagoon.

28. A *valle* house near Caposile, the small village located on the northeastern shore where the Sile River once emptied into the Lagoon.

29. Looking through the window of a Val Dogà house on an overcast day in February.

30, 31. Dinner in a house in the Val Dogà consists of fish caught in the Lagoon, bread made from locally grown wheat, and wine from island vineyards. Numerous vineyards once grew on the Lagoon's *barene*. Today's island wines are usually named after their grape: Merlot or Cabernet for red, Pinot Grigio or Tokai for white, and Clinton, an American grape, for a strong red wine popular on Murano.

32. A November sunset with stake nets and the *cogoli*, or sleeve nets, used off the Lido at Malamocco.

33. Stake nets and *cogoli* sleeve nets set out among the *barene* of the Valle del Cornio, the center of the southernmost of the Lagoon's three tidal basins.

34. The *velme, barene,* and deep-water channels at Lio Piccolo, a Lagoon village on an island whose fields are cultivated with vegetables and other produce.

35. Sea lavender blooming in August in the della Rosa marsh between Torcello and the shore, near the site of ancient Altinum.

36. A newly ploughed field in the Valle Figheri with a young crop of winter wheat and rows of maize ready for the harvest.

37. Maize, or *grano turco,* drying in a granary near Caposile on the edge of the northern Lagoon.

38, 39. Beans are harvested in August in the fields behind the village of Lio Piccolo and then separated and graded for market.

40. A light fog covers a field of artichokes on the island of Mazzorbetto near Torcello.

41. Sant'Erasmo's artichokes are here harvested during rainy weather in May. Venetian artichokes are gathered young before the choke is fully grown; once cooked, they are eaten whole.

42. A woman of Lio Piccolo drinking an afternoon coffee. Coffee was first drunk in Venice as a medicine; it then became so popular that Europe's first café was opened in the city.

43. Afternoon light illuminates the entrance of a house in the village of Lio Piccolo.

44. After fish, the staple of the Venetian diet is poultry. A woman plucks a hen on the threshing floor of her farm at Lio Piccolo.

45. Grading and crating tomatoes for market after the August harvest on Lio Piccolo.

46. In August, *anguria,* or "watermelon," is sold everywhere in the Lagoon. Watermelon markets cluster on the Lido near the fields of Treporti where the fruit is grown.

47. A bank of characteristic Mediterranean oleander in full flower near Lio Piccolo in August.

48. Marsh grass, *barene,* and channels in March with a *valle* house near Lio Piccolo in the background.

49. The beginning of the canal that divides the island of Mazzorbo in two parts. Mazzorbo once had three parishes and as many monasteries. Now only Santa Caterina remains.

50. An aerial view of Burano with the church of San Martino in the foreground. On the northern edge of the island, the long wooden footbridge links Burano with Mazzorbo.

51. The tower of Santa Caterina on Mazzorbo was built in 1318 and still has its original bell, one of the oldest surviving in Europe.

Notes on the Photographs

52. The passenger cabin of the Number 12 Vaporetto, part of the water-bus service linking Venice with Murano, Mazzorbo, Burano, Torcello, and Treporti on the Lido.

53. A fisherman rows cross-wristed—*alla valesana* ("in the manner of the *valli*")—in the Burano channel past the cathedral church and belltower of Torcello.

54. The original surface of the Via Popilia near Altinum (Altino). Few fragments of original Roman paving survive in the Veneto, because the ancient roadbeds have often been remade to serve as the province's highways.

55. Incised profile of a man on a fragment of 18th-century Venetian pottery recovered from the Lagoon.

56. The sanctuary of Torcello Cathedral. The *opus tesselatum* mosaic floor was laid in the 11th century. Behind the altar stands the bishop's throne, flanked by tiered seats for his clergy. Also lining the concave wall of the apse are marble slabs and mosaic portraits of the twelve Apostles.

57. Set in the middle of the nave floor of Torcello Cathedral is the 15th-century tombstone of Paolo d'Altino, bishop of Torcello.

58. Children play hide-and-seek in the arcaded porch of Torcello's 12th-century church dedicated to Santa Fosca.

59. A detail of Hell in the vast west-wall mosaic of Torcello Cathedral. The lustful burning in the fire of their passions and the skulls of the envious, with snakes issuing from their eyesockets, are among the best-preserved sections of mosaics now thought to have been done around 1100.

60, 61. *Fondamentie,* or canal-side quays, on Burano in the light of an overcast March day.

62, 63. The painted houses of Burano brighten the winter scene in the Lagoon islands. Old weathered brick walls, quiet narrow streets, or paved paths with glimpses of freshly colored houses at every corner typify Burano's picturesque character.

64. An old woman muffled against the cold, bright February days on Burano.

65. Weather-beaten plaster, sunny squares, and dark *calli,* or "streets," contrast with Burano's newly painted houses.

66. A striped curtain covers a front door open to spring breezes. The projecting chimney indicates that a deep hearth dominates the main room of this small Burano house.

67. Even on the façades of Burano's poorest houses, the doors and windows are outlined in white plaster imitating the stone frames of richer dwellings.

68, 69. Venetian lace, always made on Burano, became fashionable in the 16th century, only to attract competition in Brussels and elsewhere in Europe. Few natives still make the famous lace, which, according to legend, was first created out of sea foam by the Queen of the Sirens as a wedding veil for a Burano bride.

70. An eel pot or trap dries in the sun with an 18th-century house across the Mazzorbo canal in the background.

71. Eel pots and the *cogoli* sleeve nets hang from stakes along the shores of Mazzorbo.

72. A transport barge, set out with picnic table and chairs, takes its owner's family to a Sunday regatta near Burano.

73. The Lagoon's gaff-rigged sailing boats, now used for sport, are called *sampierote* after the Lido fishing village of San Pietro in Volta. Talismans against the evil eye are painted on the bow.

74. A regatta of sailing boats with the painted and patterned sails that once identified the islands and family clans of the Lagoon fishermen.

75. Pastel-colored *gondolini*—slightly built racing gondolas—compete in the Burano regatta as they race towards Torcello.

76, 77. Thousands of boats participate each year in the *Vogalonga*, the 20-mile rowing marathon in the Lagoon. An old lady watches the smaller boats, while a *peata*, or transport barge fitted for sixteen oarsmen, trails the banner of San Marco from the stern flagstaff.

78, 79. San Francesco del Deserto was the refuge of Saint Francis of Assisi in 1220. The original church on the island was built in the year of his canonization, which made it the first church anywhere dedicated to Saint Francis. Between 1420 and 1453 malaria made the island uninhabitable and emptied the monastery for a generation—whence the name *del Deserto*.

80. A lone fishing boat on the Val Dogà on a May morning.

Notes on the Photographs

81. The Number 12 Vaporetto runs along in the *bricole*-marked, deep-water channel leading to Burano. The water buses powered by steam *(vapore)* were introduced in the Lagoon in 1875.

82. A glass-factory landing stage on Murano's Grand Canal. The belltower of the island's cathedral, Santa Maria e San Donato, rises over the distant rooftops.

83. Murano's broad Grand Canal is crossed by the *ponte lungo,* an iron bridge erected in the 19th century.

84–86. Santa Maria e San Donato, Murano's 12th-century cathedral, is unique. Facing a small canal that flows from the *canal grande,* its arcaded galleries, carved-stone details, and general air of opulence belie the Byzantine and Oriental influence constant in Venetian building. Its columns, capitals, and stonework are—in part—fragments of older mainland buildings dismantled at the time of the barbarian invasions.

87. The most widely used stone in the Venetian islands was quarried across the Adriatic in Istria (today Yugoslavia). Carved milky-white Istrian stone serves for wellheads, door frames, and the balustrades of the city's many bridges.

88. A *sottoportico,* or "underpassage," typical of Venetian streets, but also found on Murano and on the Lagoon's other more built-up islands.

89. Stray cats wander about all the Lagoon's city streets, and proliferate in an infinte variety of colors and sizes.

90, 91. The pipes used for blowing Murano glass have an insulated hand grip near the mouthpiece. The master blower usually works seated near the furnace where an apprentice brings him the pipe tipped with a globule ("gather") of molten glass. The malleable glass is blown, then stretched and twisted into the desired shape. Glass can be transferred from another pipe to make stems, handles, or other appendages.

92. A wine jug made of Murano glass iridized in conscious imitation of ancient Roman glass.

93. A seated master works a blown "paraison" of molten glass, constantly turning his blowpipe in order to ensure the future object's symmetry. The pincers, shears, and other instruments used to shape the glass are dipped into a water bucket for cooling.

94–96. San Michele, Venice's cemetery island. The part nearest the city was once the separate island of San Cristoforo, but in the 19th century the two monastery islands of San Michele and San Cristoforo were joined to make the present necropolis. Now the neo-Gothic wall was built, enclosing several acres of burial ground planted with tall cypress trees. Mausolea laden with sculpture and inscribed wall tombs surround the stretches of grass and plain crosses marking the graves of the poor. The 15th-century church of San Michele and its handsome bell tower stand out clearly from the Murano end of the island.

97. Luxury hotels and their broad, sandy beaches line the Lido seashore. On the Lagoon side languishes the abandoned quarantine island of the old Lazzaretto, while in the distance Poveglia partly hides a grounded oil tanker.

98. As we look across from the Lido to the basin of San Marco and the city of Venice, San Giorgio's dome and slender tower seem much closer than the massive campanile rising above the pink mass of the Doges' Palace.

99. *Bricole* mark the channel for a tanker heading out to sea through the San Nicolò sea entrance.

100–103, 106–111. The Excelsior Hotel at the Lido was built in 1906. A *belle époque* fantasy, it boasts a pseudo-Moorish exterior and many rooms embellished in the grandiose style associated with César Ritz. The vast complex, which is owned by CIGA, Italy's luxury hotel chain, offers a large beach covered with elegant, white cabañas, an immense swimming pool, and indoor as well as outdoor restaurants. The beach makes the perfect setting for sybaritic life from May through September. It once served as the center of Venice's famous film festival, which every September brought stars from all over the world. Pretty girls still soak up the sun, some stars continue to breakfast on their terraces (109), and tourists glutted with Venice's art come out for a swim.

104–105. The beach and jetty of the Grand Hôtel des Bains. The thatched-roof cabañas—a touch of Acapulco—were erected after the tidal wave of November 1966 had swept away the old bathing cabins. The slight variation in the pier's evident height indicates that the water is only about 7 feet deep at the end. An historic site, the hotel was where the great impressario Serge de Diaghilev died in 1929. And it was on the hotel's beach that Aschenbach, the hero of Thomas Mann's *Death in Venice,* died enthralled by the vision of the Polish boy Tadzio.

112. Venice's golf course lies at the southern end of the Lido surrounded by the ruined walls of the Alberoni fortress.

Notes on the Photographs

113, 114.   There is stabling for horses on the Lido, and the grand hotels sponsor an equestrian club with occasional jumping competitions. The Lido's riding club follows the bridal path along the *murazzi*, the island's 18th-century seawalls.

115.   Standing on the bow of a lifeguard's boat, two boys watch members of the equestrian club out for a morning ride on the beach.

116.   An oil tanker in mothballs lies aground in the Lagoon shallows not far from the Alberoni end of the Lido.

117.   Another giant tanker lies aground and abandoned nearer the fishing village of Malamocco.

118.   A Franciscan friar rides his bicycle on a May morning near the ancient church of San Nicolò del Lido.

119.   The Jewish burial ground on the Lido is the oldest cemetery in the Lagoon. It contains tombs of Venetian Jews buried there as far back as the mid-14th century.

120.   The ruined and deserted monastery island of San Giorgio in Alega ("Saint George in the Seaweed") once constituted an important Benedictine community. It was the first island on the channel linking the mainland with Venice.

121.   A dock for small boats at the Lido fishing port of Malamocco provides a view across the sunset Lagoon toward the smokestacks of the refineries at Marghera.

122.   A cluster of *bricole* piling marks a navigable channel.

123.   Trawl nets being hauled aboard by two fishermen just off Alberoni. A line of mussel nurseries marks the faint horizon.

124.   Healthy green algae spread over *velme*, the Lagoon's sandy shoals exposed at low tide.

125.   *Bricole* channel markers off Malamocco in the evening before sunset.

126.   The bell tower of San Lazzaro, the island whose Armenian monks Lord Byron visited during his Venetian sojourn.

127.   Sunset reflections of *bricole* channel markers in the Lagoon.

128. Two small boats tacking across the Lagoon in a regatta off the Lido.

129. Fishing boats at sea off the Lido in the early morning.

130. Waves from the Adriatic break on the rock-strewn shore of San Pietro in Volta. Tall hedgerows protect vegetable garden plots planted on the narrow littoral.

131. Pellestrina is the principal fishing town on the littoral south of the Lido. Rocks line the shore as a foundation for the *murazzi*, or seawalls, built to protect the town.

132. Locally harvested cane shelters rows of delicate young vegetables from sea storms and salt wind at San Pietro in Volta.

133. Reed windbrakes and netting against birds protect the plantings of San Pietro in Volta's market gardens.

134. A rainy day on the quay at Pellestrina. In the background a wooden shack built on stilts in the Lagoon is used for cleaning the harvest from the mussel nurseries.

135. Pellestrina's harbor with brightly painted trawlers tied up at the quay.

136. Crowds line the Pellestrina quay to watch the finish of the two-man *sandolo* race in the annual August regatta.

137. Fishermen's boats from all over the Lagoon arrive with their families and friends to cheer local favorites in the Pellestrina regatta.

138. The heavy curved bow of the Lagoon's typical fishing boat, the *bragozzo*, is painted with talismans and symbols to ward off the evil eye and bring the luck needed for a good catch.

139. A woman of Pellestrina is wrapped in a shawl of a type still crocheted throughout the Lagoon. Such work varies in pattern and color according to the individual community.

140. A *trattoria* set out under the trees at Malamocco on the Lido.

141. Lunch in a restaurant at Pellestrina on an August weekend.

142. Children play in the sea-blasted fields at Pellestrina. The Adriatic lies behind the embankments across the road, while in the far right an abandoned 19th-century fortress points its empty gunports out to sea.

143. Two boys going fishing ride their bicycle on the road between Malamocco and Alberoni.

Notes on the Photographs

144. Wading in the shallows to find clams near Malamocco on an April evening.

145. The *murazzi,* tall seawalls built in the 18th-century to protect the Lagoon from sea storms, are at their most impressive near the end of the Pellestrina littoral.

146. Near Chioggia's sea entrance lies the Octagon of Caroman, a 19th-century fortress island that, with three other such installations, defended the Lagoon from enemy attack.

147. The Madonna of the Fisherman, a traditional, canopy-covered Venetian shrine perched on a cluster of *bricole* near the Chioggia sea entrance. The new development of Sottomarina rises in the background.

148. Chioggia from the air, showing the city's two main arteries. Crossed by numerous bridges, the Canal Vena is crowded with fishing boats at the end of the day. Parallel to it runs the wide Corso del Popolo, a street for land traffic crossing the *ponte longa* from Sottomarina.

149. A fishing trawler heads out to sea. Behind it empty construction-transport barges ride high in the water, at the end of which appears the new city of Sottomarina.

150–154. The Chioggia port and fish market is one of the most important in Italy. Boats bring in *pesce azzura,* a local blue fish, which represents the most abundant product of the Chioggia fishing industry (152, 154). *Seppie,* the local cuttlefish, also abound (150), but only a small portion of the catch goes for local consumption. The bulk is sent elsewhere in Italy, and the remainder shipped all over Europe.

155. A fisherman crosses a bridge over the Canal Vena with the 16th-century Palazzo Grassi in the background.

156. Fishermen of Chioggia play cards in a bar at the center of the old town.

157. An examination in winter of some of the endless varieties of local red lettuce sold in Chioggia's vegetable market.

158. A giant tanker uses the newly dredged shipping canal connecting the Malamocco sea entrance with Marghera. Stake nets are set out in the foreground while, distant Monte Rua seems near at hand in the clear dusk.

159. The tall smokestacks of the Mestre-Marghera petrochemical refinery and port complex built on the edge of the Lagoon.

160. Fishermen out for clams at sunset.

Technical Notes

1
Leica R3 Telyt 560 mm.
Tripod used.
1/30–8. Kodachrome 64 ASA.

2
Leica R3 Summicron 90 mm.
1/250–5,6. Kodachrome 64 ASA.

3
Leica R3 Summicron 35 mm.
1/250–5,6. Kodachrome 64 ASA.

4
Leica R3 Summicron 90 mm.
1/1000–2.8. Kodachrome 25 ASA.

5
Leica R3 Summicron 90 mm.
1/1000–4. Kodachrome 25 ASA.

6
Leica R3 Telyt 400 mm.
1/250–5,6. Kodachrome 64 ASA.

7
Leica R3 Telyt 400 mm.
1/250–5,6. Kodachrome 64 ASA.

8
Leica R3 Telyt 800 mm.
Tripod used.
1/125–8. Kodachrome 64 ASA.

9
Leica R3 Telyt 800 mm.
Tripod used.
1/125–8. Kodachrome 64 ASA.

10
Leica R3 Telyt 400 mm.
1/500–4. Kodachrome 64 ASA.

11
Leica R3 Telyt 400 mm.
1/500–4. Kodachrome 64 ASA.

12
Leica M4-2 Summilux 35 mm.
1/250–4. Kodachrome 64 ASA.

13
Leica M4-2 Summilux 35 mm.
1/250–4. Kodachrome 25 ASA.

14
Leica R3 Summilux 50 mm.
1/250–4. Kodachrome 25 ASA.

15
Leica R3 Summicron 50 mm.
1/250–5,6. Kodachrome 64 ASA.

16
Leica M4-2 Summilux 35 mm.
Kodachrome 64 ASA.

17
Leica R3 Super Angulon 21 mm.
1/125–5,6. Kodachrome 25 ASA.

18
Leica M4 Summicron 90 mm.
1/250–5,6. Kodachrome 25 ASA.

19
Ibid.

20
Leica R3 Summicron 35 mm.
1/125–5,6. Kodachrome 64 ASA.

21
Leica M4-2 Summicron 35 mm.
1/250–4. Kodachrome 25 ASA.

22
Leica R3 Summilux 50 mm.
1/250–4. Kodachrome 64 ASA.

23
Leica R3 Summicron 35 mm.
1/125–5,6. Kodachrome 64 ASA.

24
Leica R3 Summilux 50 mm.
1/60–2. Kodachrome 25 ASA.

25
Ibid.

26
Leica R3 Summicron 90 mm.
1/250–5,6. Kodachrome 64 ASA.

27
Leica R3 Summilux 50 mm.
1/250–5,6. Kodachrome 64 ASA.

28
Leica R3 Telyt 560 mm.
Tripod used.
1/30–8. Kodachrome 25 ASA.

29
Leica R3 Summilux 50 mm.
1/125–4. Kodachrome 25 ASA.

30
Leica R3 Summicron 90 mm.
1/60–4. Ektachrome 64 ASA.

31
Ibid.

32
Leica R3 Apo-Telyt 180 mm.
1/250–5,6. Kodachrome 64 ASA.

33
Leica R3 Summicron 90 mm.
1/125–4. Kodachrome 25 ASA.

34
Leica R3 Summicron 50 mm.
1/500–4. Kodachrome 64 ASA.

35
Leica R3 Summicron 35 mm.
1/60–8. Kodachrome 25 ASA.

36
Leica R3 Elmarit 135 mm.
1/250–4. Kodachrome 25 ASA.

37
Leica M4-2 Summilux 35 mm.
1/125–4. Kodachrome 25 ASA.

38
Leica R3 Summicron 35 mm.
1/250–8. Kodachrome 25 ASA.

39
Leica M4-2 Summicron 35 mm.
1/60–5,6. Kodachrome 64 ASA.

40
Leica R3 Summicron 50 mm.
1/125–4. Kodachrome 25 ASA.

41
Leica R3 Summicron 90 mm.
1/125–4. Kodachrome 64 ASA.

42
Leica R3 Elmar 180 mm.
1/250–5,6. Kodachrome 25 ASA.

43
Leica R3 Summicron 35 mm.
1/125–5,6. Kodachrome 25 ASA.

44
Leica R3 Elmar 180 mm.
1/250–5,6. Kodachrome 25 ASA.

45
Leica R3 Summicron 35 mm.
1/250–4. Kodachrome 25 ASA.

46
Leica R3 Summicron 50 mm.
1/250–5,6. Kodachrome 25 ASA.

47
Leica R3 Summicron 25 ASA.

48
Leica R3 Summicron 90 mm.
1/250–4. Kodachrome 25 ASA.

49
Leica R3 Summicron 90 mm.
1/250–2,8. Kodachrome 64 ASA.

50
Leica R3 Summicron 50 mm.
1/500–2. Kodachrome 25 ASA.

51
Leica R3 Summilux 50 mm.
1/125–4. Kodachrome 64 ASA.

52
Leica R3 Summicron 35 mm.
1/60–4. Kodachrome 64 ASA.

53
Leica R3 Summicron 90 mm.
1/250–5,6. Kodachrome 25 ASA.

54
Leica R3 Elmar 180 mm.
1/250–8. Kodachrome 25 ASA.

55
Leica R3 Macro-Elmarit 60 mm.
1/250–8. Kodachrome 64 ASA.

56
Leica R3 Summicron 35 mm.
Tripod used.
1/15–8. Kodachrome 64 ASA.

57
Ibid.

58
Leica R3 Summicron 50 mm.
1/250–5,6. Kodachrome 64 ASA.

59
Leica R3 Elmar 180 mm.
1/30–4. Kodachrome 64 ASA.

60
Leica R3 Summicron 90 mm.
1/250–4. Kodachrome 64 ASA.

61
Leica R3 Summicron 90 mm.
1/250–5,6. Ektachrome HS 160 ASA.

62
Leica R3 Summilux 50 mm.
1/250–4. Kodachrome 25 ASA.

63
Leica R3 Summicron 90 mm.
1/250–4. Kodachrome 64 ASA.

64
Leica R3 Summicron 90 mm.
1/250–4. Kodachrome 64 ASA.

65
Leica R3 Summicron 35 mm.
1/125–5,6. Kodachrome 64 ASA.

66
Leica M4-2 Summicron 90 mm.
1/250–5,6. Kodachrome 64 ASA.

67
Ibid.

68
Leica M4-2 Summicron 50 mm.
1/125–4. Kodachrome 25 ASA.

69
Leica M4-2 Summicron 50 mm.
1/125–5,6. Kodachrome 25 ASA.

70
Leica R3 Summicron 90 mm.
1/250–5,6. Kodachrome 25 ASA.

71
Leica R3 Telyt 400mm.
1/250–5,6. Kodachrome 64 ASA.

72
Leica R3 Elmarit 90 mm.
1/250–5,6. Kodachrome 25 ASA.

73
Leica R3 Apo-Telyt 180 mm.
1/250–5,6. Kodachrome 25 ASA.

74
Leica R3 Summicron 35 mm.
1/250–8. Kodachrome 64 ASA.

75
Leica R3 Elmarit 135 mm
1/500–5,6. Kodachrome 64 ASA.

76
Leica R3 Elmarit 24 mm.
1/250–8. Kodachrome 64 ASA.

77
Leica R3 Apo-Telyt 180 mm.
1/250–5,6. Kodachrome 64 ASA.

78
Leica R3 Summicron 50 mm.
1/500–4. Kodachrome 25 ASA.

79
Leica R3 Elmarit 24 mm.
1/125–8. Kodachrome 25 ASA.

80
Leica R3 Apo-Telyt 180 mm.
1/250–8. Kodachrome 25 ASA.

81
Leica R3 Summicron 50 mm.
1/1000–2. Kodachrome 25 ASA.

82
Leica Super Angulon 21 mm.
1/250–5,6. Kodachrome 25 ASA.

83
Leica R3 Elmar 180 mm.
1/500–4. Kodachrome 25 ASA.

84
Leica R3 Super Angulon 21 mm.
1/60–8. Kodachrome 25 ASA.

85
Leica R3 Apo-Telyt 180 mm.
1/125–5,6. Kodachrome 64 ASA.

86
Ibid.

87
Leica R3 Summicron 90 mm.
1/250–5,6. Kodachrome 25 ASA.

88
Leica R3 Summicron 90 mm.
1/250–5,6. Kodachrome 25 ASA.

89
Leica R3 Elmarit 135 mm.
1/125–4. Kodachrome 25 ASA.

90
Leica R3 Summilux 50 mm.
1/60–2. Kodachrome 64 ASA.

91
Ibid.

92
Leica R3 Macro Elmarit 60 mm.
1/60–8. Kodachrome 64 ASA.

93
Leica R3 Summilux 50 mm.
1/60–4. Kodachrome 64 ASA.

94
Leica R3 Super Angulon 21 mm.
1/125–8. Kodachrome 64 ASA.

95
Leica R3 Apo-Telyt 180 mm.
1/125–5,6. Kodachrome 64 ASA.

96
Leica R3 Super Angulon 21 mm.
1/500–4. Kodachrome 25 ASA.

97
Leica R3 Summicron 50 mm.
1/500–4. Kodachrome 64 ASA.

98
Leica R3 Elmarit 135 mm.
1/250–4. Kodachrome 64 ASA.

99
Leica M4-2 Summilux 35 mm.
1/125–5,6. Kodachrome 64 ASA.

100
Leica R3 Elmar 180 mm.
1/250–8. Kodachrome 25 ASA.

101
Leica R3 Summicron 90 mm.
1/500–5,6. Kodachrome 25 ASA.

102
Leica R3 Elmarit 135 mm.
1/250–5,6. Kodachrome 25 ASA.

103
Leica R3 Summilux 50 mm.
1/125–4. Kodachrome 25 ASA.

104
Leica R3 Summicron 90 mm.
1/1000–2,8. Kodachrome 25 ASA.

105
Leica R3 Elmarit 135 mm.
1/1000–4. Kodachrome 64 ASA.

106
Leica R3 Summicron 35 mm.
1/250–4, Kodachrome 25 ASA.

107
Leica R3 Summicron 90 mm.
1/250–4. Kodachrome 25 ASA.

108
Leica R3 Elmar 180 mm.
1/500–4. Kodachrome 64 ASA.

109
Leica SL2 Summilux 50 mm.
1/250–4. Kodachrome 25 ASA.

110
Leica SL2 Summicron 35 mm.
1/60–4. Kodachrome 64 ASA.

111
Leica M4-2 Noctilus 50 mm.
1/125–1. Ektachrome Type B 160 ASA.

112
Leica R3 Apo-Telyt 180 mm.
1/250–4. Kodachrome 25 ASA.

113
Leica SL2 Summilux 50 mm.
1/125–4. Kodachrome 25 ASA.

114
Leica M4-2 Summicron 90 mm.
1/250–5,6. Kodachrome 64 ASA.

115
Leica M4-2 Summicron 50 mm.
1/250–5,6. Kodachrome 64 ASA.

116
Leica R3 Elmar 180 mm.
1/250–5,6. Kodachrome 64 ASA.

117
Leica R3 Elmar 180 mm.
1/250–5,6. Kodachrome 64 ASA.

118
Leica R3 Summicron 90 mm.
1/250–n2. Kodachrome 64 ASA.

119
Leica R3 Summilux 50 mm.
1/250–1,4. Kodachrome 200 ASA.

120
Leica R3 Summicron 50 mm.
1/500–4. Kodachrome 25 ASA.

121
Leica M4-2. Summicron 50 mm.
1/500–4. Kodachrome 25 ASA.

122
Leica SL2 Elmar 180 mm.
1/250–5,6. Kodachrome 25 ASA.

123
Leica R3 Elmar 180 mm.
1/250–4. Kodachrome 64 ASA.

Technical Notes

124
Leica R3 Summicron 35 mm.
1/250–4. Kodachrome 25 ASA.

125
Leica R3 Summicron 35 mm.
1/125–5,6. Kodachrome 25 ASA.

126
Leica M4-2 Summilux 35 mm.
1/125–5,6. Kodachrome 25 ASA.

127
Leica R3 Telyt 560 mm.
1/125–8. Kodachrome 64 ASA.

128
Leica R3 Summicron 50 mm.
1/1000–4. Kodachrome 25 ASA.

129
Leica R3 Apo-Telyt 180 mm.
1/500–5,6. Kodachrome 25 ASA.

130
Leica M4-2 Summicron 90 mm.
1/500–4. Kodachrome 25 ASA.

131
Leica M4-2 Summicron 50 mm.
1/500–4. Kodachrome 25 ASA.

132
Leica R3 Summicron 90 mm.
1/250–4. Kodachrome 64 ASA.

133
Ibid.

134
Leica M4-2 Summilux 35 mm.
1/125–4. Kodachrome 64 ASA.

135
Leica M4-2 Summilux 35 mm.
1/250–5,6.

136
Leica R3 Elmar 180 mm.
1/250–4. Kodachrome 64 ASA.

137
Leica R3 Elmar 180 mm.
1/500–4. Kodachrome 64 ASA.

138
Leica R3 Summicron 90 mm.
1/250–4. Kodachrome 64 ASA.

139
Leica R3 Summicron 35 mm.
1/125–5,6. Kodachrome 25 ASA.

140
Leica R3 Summilux 50 mm.
1/250–4. Kodachrome 25 ASA.

141
Leica M4-2 Summicron 50 mm.
1/250–5,6. Kodachrome 25 ASA.

142
Leica R3 Summilux 50 mm.
1/250–4. Ektachrome 64 ASA.

143
Leica R3 Summicron 90 mm.
1/250–4. Kodachrome 25 ASA.

144
Leica R3 Summilux 50 mm.
1/125–4. Kodachrome 64 ASA.

145
Leica M4-2 Summicron 90 mm.
1/500–5,6. Kodachrome 25 ASA.

146
Leica R3 Elmarit 135 mm.
1/500–4. Kodachrome 25 ASA.

147
Leica R3 Elmar 180 mm.
1/500–4. Kodachrome 25 ASA.

148
Leica R3 Summicron 90 mm.
1/500–4. Kodachrome 25 ASA.

149
Leica R3 Elmarit 135 mm.
1/250–5,6. Kodachrome 25 ASA.

150
Leica R3 Summilux 50 mm.
1/125–4. Kodachrome 64 ASA.

151
Leica M4-2 Summilux 35 mm.
1/60–4. Kodachrome 64 ASA.

152
Leica R3 Elmarit 135 mm.
1/125–4. Kodachrome 64 ASA.

153
Leica R3 Summilux 50 mm.
1/125–4. Kodachrome 64 ASA.

154
Leica R3 Summicron 35 mm.
1/250–5,6. Kodachrome 25 ASA.

155
Leica R3 Summilux 50 mm.
1/250–4. Kodachrome 64 ASA.

157
Leica R3 Summicron 90 mm.
1/250–4. Kodachrome 25 ASA.

158
Leica R3 Telyt 560 mm.
Tripod used.
1/125–8. Kodachrome 64 ASA.

159
Leica R3 Elmar 180 mm.
1/1000–4. Kodachrome 25 ASA.

160
Leica R3 Telyt 560 mm.
1/60–8. Kodachrome 64 ASA.

207